COCKROACHES

INSECTS IN MY BACKYARD

RYAN JAMES

NORWOOD HOUSE PRESS

Library of Congress Cataloging-in-Publication Data

Names: James, Ryan.
Title: Cockroaches / Ryan James.
Description: Buffalo, NY : Norwood House Press, 2025. | Series: Insects in my backyard | Includes glossary and index.
Identifiers: ISBN 9781684502561 (pbk.) | ISBN 9781684502578 (library bound) | ISBN 9781684502585 (ebook)
Subjects: LCSH: Cockroaches--Juvenile literature.
Classification: LCC QL505.5 J359 2025 | DDC 595.7'28--dc23

Published in 2025 by
Norwood House Press
2544 Clinton Street
Buffalo, NY 14224

Designer: Ocean Books
Editor: Kim Thompson

Photo credits: Cover, p. 1 luis2499/Shutterstock.com; p. 5 skifbook/Shutterstock.com; p. 6-7 gan chaonan/Shutterstock.com; p. 9 supasart meekumari/Shutterstock.com; p. 10 guentermanaus/Shutterstock.com; p. 11 Guillermo Guerao Serra/Shutterstock.com; p. 12 Liz weber/Shutterstock.com; p. 13 Alexey Stiop/Shutterstock.com; p. 15 Zairia Zmal/Shutterstock.com; p. 16 Hafiez Razali/Shutterstock.com; p. 17 RHJPhotos/Shutterstock.com; p. 19 Portographer/Shutterstock.com; p. 21 Aastels/Shutterstock.com

Printed in the United States of America

CPSIA compliance information: Batch #CW25NHP: For further information contact Norwood House Press at 1-800-237-9932.

TABLE OF CONTENTS

WHAT IS A COCKROACH?

Cockroaches are **insects** you might see in your backyard. They come out at night to find food and water.

BODY PARTS

A cockroach's flat body helps it hide in small spaces. Its **exoskeleton** is a hard shell that provides protection.

Cockroaches have long **antennae** on their heads. The antennae help them find food and sense danger.

Cockroaches have six long legs. Their legs help them run away quickly from **predators**.

TYPES OF COCKROACHES

The American cockroach is found in the United States. It is large and reddish-brown. It likes warm, damp places like basements and **sewers**.

The German cockroach is found in Europe. It is small and light brown with two dark stripes on its back. It is often found in kitchens and bathrooms.

The Oriental cockroach is commonly found in Asia. It is dark and shiny. It prefers cool, damp areas under rocks and logs.

The brown-banded cockroach is often seen in Africa. It has light brown bands across its wings. It can be found in warm, dry places.

COCKROACH BEHAVIOR

Cockroaches come out at night to look for food. They eat almost anything, including leaves and small insects.

During the day, cockroaches hide in dark, damp places. They like to stay under rocks and logs and in piles of leaves.

Cockroaches move quickly when they feel **threatened**. They run away to find new hiding spots.

WHY ARE COCKROACHES IMPORTANT?

Cockroaches are **decomposers**. When they eat, they break down dead plants and animals. This helps keep the ground clean and the soil healthy.

Cockroaches are food for many animals like birds and lizards. They are an important part of the food chain.

Cockroaches can teach us about **survival**. They have been around for millions of years. They can live in almost any environment.

GLOSSARY

antennae (an-TEN-ee): slender, movable, segmented organs on the heads of insects that are used to sense the environment; feelers

decomposers (dee-kuhm-POH-zurz): living things, such as insects, bacteria, or mushrooms, that feed on and break down dead plants and animals

exoskeleton (EK-soh-skel-uh-tuhn): a hard supporting structure on the outside of the body, as on insects, spiders, and crustaceans

insects (IN-sekts): small animals that have hard outer skeletons instead of backbones and that have three pairs of legs, one or two pairs of wings, and three body sections

predators (PRED-uh-turz): animals that live by hunting other animals for food

sewers (SOO-urz): underground pipes that carry away drainage water and liquid and solid waste

survival (sur-VYE-vuhl): continuing to live

threatened (THRE-tuhnd): in danger of being harmed

THINKING QUESTIONS

1. Name three cockroach body parts.
2. How are an American cockroach and a German cockroach alike and different?
3. How do antennae help cockroaches?
4. What animals eat cockroaches?
5. Why are cockroaches important?

INDEX

ABOUT THE AUTHOR

Ryan James lives in the western part of North Carolina with his rescue dog Bailey. As a child, he would search for creepy crawlies as he hiked through the forest near his house. When he's not on the hiking or biking trail, he is cheering on his favorite baseball and football teams.